COOKING WITH
HERBS & SPICES

Photography by Peter Barry
Designed by Richard Hawke and Claire Leighton
Edited by Jillian Stewart and Kate Cranshaw
Recipes by Judith Ferguson, Lalita Ahmed and
    Carolyn Garner

3451
© 1993 Coombe Books
This edition published in 1993 by Coombe Books
for Parragon Book Service Ltd.,
707 High Road, Finchley, London N12 0BT
All rights reserved.
Printed in Hong Kong
ISBN 1-85813-381-5

COOKING WITH HERBS & SPICES

PARRAGON

Contents

Introduction

Herbs and spices have been used as invaluable cooking aids throughout culinary history and, whilst they are of little nutritional importance, their contribution to our diet in terms of scent, flavour, and colour is enormous. Not only do they have unusual properties which can develop the taste of other ingredients or 'tone' down rich or fatty flavours, they also aid digestion and even freshen the breath.

The flavour of a herb comes from essential oils in the leaves, stems and flowers, which, when crushed or heated, release the herbs particular flavour. In general, a herb is green and leafy and can be used fresh or dried, while a spice is the dried – sometimes ground – seeds, pods, berries, roots, stems, or bark of a plant. Many plants are used as both a herb and a spice. Coriander, for example, is extremely versatile and is used ground in Indian cuisine, while its leaf is often found in herb salads.

Freshly picked herbs have a wonderful flavour, and should be used in preference to dried whenever possible. When buying fresh herbs, choose the bushiest and brightest in colour, avoiding limp stems and discoloured or drooping leaves. Fresh herbs will keep for several days in the refrigerator, and are best stored in the salad drawer wrapped in damp kitchen paper and placed in an open plastic bag. Living herbs can now be bought from many large supermarkets, and will keep quite happily on a sunny window-sill, so even if you don't have a garden you should still have access to fresh herbs of one sort or another.

Dried herbs, although not as good as fresh, are still an excellent store cupboard stand-by. Some herbs dry better than others, particularly the woody herbs such as bay leaves, thyme, marjoram, and rosemary. Delicate herbs such as chervil, tarragon, and basil do not keep their characteristic scents and flavours very well, but they will freeze better, and can be sealed in bags and then crumbled, or chopped and packed into ice-cube trays with a little water. When using dried herbs in place of fresh, remember to halve the quantity, as dried herbs have a more concentrated flavour. The flavour of herbs is most characteristic when raw, hence their addition to salads, uncooked sauces, and dressings. However, some herbs – notably rosemary and thyme – benefit from long cooking as they impart their flavours slowly. Other delicate herbs, such as basil, chervil, tarragon and parsley, should be added towards the end of the cooking as their essential oils are particularly volatile and their flavours quickly disperse.

Using over 40 different herbs and spices, this book perfectly illustrates the wonderful qualities of many of our favourite herbs and spices. There are recipes for all occasions covering starters, main courses, side dishes and desserts, all of which will tempt the cook into creating new and exciting dishes using herbs and spices.

CARROT AND BASIL SOUP

Carrots and basil make a wonderful combination in this delicious soup.

SERVES 4

45g/1½oz butter or margarine
2 shallots, finely chopped
6 carrots, peeled and diced
2 large potatoes, peeled and diced
1150ml/2 pints chicken or vegetable stock
570ml/1 pint water
2 tbsps chopped basil
1 bay leaf
Pinch nutmeg
Juice of ½ lemon
Salt and pepper
140ml/¼ pint cream

Garnish
Fresh basil leaves

1. Melt the butter or margarine in a heavy-based pan and cook the shallots over a gentle heat to soften.
2. Add the carrots and potatoes and cook for 2 minutes, stirring occasionally.
3. Add the stock, water, basil, bay leaf, nutmeg, lemon juice, salt and pepper and cook 20-25 minutes.
4. When the vegetables are tender remove the bay leaf and allow the soup to cool slightly.
5. Purée in a food processor or blender and add the cream.
6. Reheat gently and garnish with the fresh basil leaves.

TIME: Preparation takes 25 minutes and cooking takes about 25 minutes.

WATCHPOINT: Do not allow the soup to boil once the cream has been added.

SERVING IDEAS: Serve with crusty wholemeal bread.

SPICY CHILLI BEAN SOUP

This 'complete meal' soup certainly doesn't need salt to bring out the full flavour of the ingredients.

SERVES 4-6

3 tbsps vegetable oil

2 onions, roughly chopped

1 clove garlic, crushed

1 tbsp ground cumin

2 tsps ground paprika

1 red or green chilli, seeded and finely
   chopped

225g/8oz minced beef

790g/1¾lbs canned tomatoes, chopped

850ml/1½ pints chicken or vegetable stock

90g/3oz tomato purée

1 tsp fresh oregano leaves

1 bay leaf

140ml/¼ pint beer

Freshly ground black pepper

120g/4oz each of canned red kidney beans,
   chick peas, and white pinto beans,
   drained and thoroughly rinsed

1. Heat the oil in a large, heavy-based saucepan.

2. Add the onion and garlic and cook slowly until they become transparent.

3. Stir in the cumin, paprika and chilli. Increase the heat and cook quickly for 30 seconds, stirring all the time.

4. Add the meat and cook until lightly browned, breaking up any large pieces with a fork.

5. Add the tomatoes and their juice, the stock, tomato purée, oregano, bay leaf, beer and pepper. Stir well, then bring to the boil.

6. Cover and simmer for approximately 50 minutes, checking the level of liquid several times during the cooking and adding more water if the soup seems too dry.

7. During the last 15 minutes of cooking, add the drained beans, stirring them in to mix well.

TIME: Preparation takes 30 minutes, cooking takes 1 hour.

COOK'S TIP: If you cannot buy canned beans and chick peas, use 60g/2oz each of dried beans. Soak them overnight and cook thoroughly for 1 hour before using in this recipe.

SERVING IDEAS: Serve with a mixed garnish of chopped fresh tomatoes, chopped spring onions and cubed avocado which has been sprinkled with lemon juice.

Gravad Laks with Mustard Dill Sauce

This traditional Scandinavian dish makes a delicious starter.

SERVES 6-8

450g/1lb filleted centre cut of fresh salmon, unskinned
1 tbsp coarsely ground sea salt
12 crushed white peppercorns
2 tbsps sugar
3 tbsps chopped fresh dill
½ tsp crushed allspice berries
2 tbsps brandy

Sauce

1 tbsp strong mustard, such as Dijon
1 tbsp sweet Swedish-style mustard
1 tbsp sugar
1 tbsp oil
2 tsps white wine vinegar
Salt and pepper
1 tbsp chopped fresh dill

1. Remove as many of the small bones as possible from the salmon. Rinse the fish and pat dry.

2. Combine salt, peppercorns, sugar, dill and allspice and rub evenly onto each piece of salmon on the flesh side.

3. Sprinkle the brandy over each side and press the two sides together, skin side outermost.

4. Wrap tightly in foil. Place in a shallow dish and weight down the top of the fish. Leave for 24-36 hours in the refrigerator. Turn the parcel several times and weigh down after each turning.

5. Scrape off most of the dill and spices and slice the fish on a slant, across the grain, into very thin slices. Discard the skin.

6. To prepare the sauce, combine the mustards and sugar. Gradually add the oil in a thin, steady stream, whisking constantly.

7. Add the vinegar gradually, to thin slightly; the sauce should be the consistency of thick cream.

8. Season with salt and pepper and add more sugar or vinegar if wished. Stir in the dill and serve with the gravad laks.

TIME: Preparation takes 15 minutes plus 1–2 days marinating.

BUYING GUIDE: Make sure that you buy 2 pieces of salmon, from either side of the backbone so that they can be sandwiched together before marinating.

SERVING IDEAS: Serve with brown bread and butter.

DOLMADES

In Greece, stuffed vine leaves are not served with a tomato sauce. Try a light egg-lemon sauce (see recipe for Stuffed Courgettes), or natural yogurt instead.

SERVES 6-8

225g/8oz fresh vine leaves or leaves packed
    in brine
175g/6oz long-grain rice, cooked
8 spring onions, finely chopped
1½ tbsps chopped fresh dill
3 tbsps chopped fresh mint
1 tbsp chopped fresh parsley
60g/2oz pine nuts
60g/2oz currants
Salt and pepper
140ml/¼ pint olive oil
Juice of 1 lemon

1. If using fresh vine leaves, put them into boiling water for about 1 minute. Remove them and drain. If using preserved vine leaves, rinse them and then place in a bowl of hot water for 5 minutes to soak. Strain and pat dry.

2. Mix together all the remaining ingredients except the olive oil and lemon juice. Taste the filling and adjust the seasoning if necessary.

3. Spread the vine leaves out on a flat surface, vein side upwards. Cut off the stems and place about 2 tsps, of filling on each leaf, pressing it into a sausage shape.

4. Fold the sides of the leaves over to partially cover the stuffing and roll up as for a Swiss roll. Place the rolls seam side down in a large saucepan. Pour over the olive oil and lemon juice.

5. Pour hot water over the rolls until it comes about halfway up their sides. Set a plate on top of the rolls to keep them in place, cover the pan and cook slowly for about 40 minutes.

6. Remove the Dolmades to a serving plate and accompany with lemon wedges, black olives and natural yogurt, if wished.

TIME: Preparation takes about 30 minutes, cooking takes about 40 minutes.

VARIATIONS: Other ingredients may be used in the filling. Substitute chopped olives, almonds or chopped cooked lamb.

PREPARATION: Dolmades may be prepared a day before serving. Leave in their liquid in the refrigerator and reheat just before serving, or serve cold.

PRAWNS IN MELON

Deliciously cool and refreshing for a summer lunch, this recipe could also be served as an unusual starter for eight people.

SERVES 4

2 small melons
4 medium tomatoes
1 small cucumber
1 orange
Juice of ½ a lemon
60ml/4 tbsps light vegetable oil
3 tbsps double cream
2 tbsps chopped fresh mint, reserve
    4 sprigs for garnish
Pinch of sugar
Salt and pepper
1 tsp chopped fresh lemon thyme
225g/8oz peeled prawns
90g/3oz toasted flaked almonds

1. Cut the melons in half through the middle, remove the seeds and scoop out the flesh with a melon baller, or spoon. Leave a 5mm/¼-inch border of fruit on the inside of each shell.

2. Cut the melon flesh into 1cm/½-inch cubes, or leave in balls. Skin the tomatoes and remove the seeds. Cut the flesh into strips. Peel the cucumber, cut in half lengthways and then into 1cm/½-inch cubes. Peel and segment the orange.

3. In a large bowl, mix together the lemon juice, oil and double cream. Stir in the mint, sugar, salt and pepper and thyme. Add the prawns and the fruit and vegetables, and mix thoroughly to coat evenly with the dressing.

4. Pile equal quantities of the fruit and prawn mixture into the melon shells and chill well.

5. Serve garnished with the reserved mint sprigs and the almonds.

TIME: Preparation takes about 25 minutes. Allow at least 2 hours for chilling the salad, before serving.

PREPARATION: If the melon shells will not stand upright, cut a thin slice off the bottom of each one to make them more stable.

SERVING IDEAS: Serve with a mixed green salad and new potatoes.

CHEESE AND VINE LEAVES

An unusual starter which is certain to impress and delight your guests.

SERVES 4

4 pieces goat's or feta cheese
280ml/½ pint olive oil
60ml/4 tbsps chopped fresh herbs such as
    basil, tarragon, oregano, marjoram,
    parsley
2 cloves garlic, crushed (optional)
Squeeze lemon juice
1 bay leaf

To Serve
4 fresh vine leaves, washed, or 4 brine-
    packed vine leaves, soaked 30 minutes
1 head radicchio
8 leaves curly endive, washed and torn in
    bite-size pieces

1. If using goat's cheese, make sure it is not too ripe. Lightly score the surface of whichever cheese is used.

2. Mix together the oil, herbs, garlic, lemon juice and bay leaf. Place the cheese in a small, deep bowl or jar and pour over the oil mixture. If cheese is not completely covered, pour on more oil.

3. Leave, covered, overnight in the refrigerator. Drain the cheese, reserving the marinade, and place in a hinged wire rack, if available. Grill the cheese over hot coals, or under a grill, until light golden brown and just beginning to melt.

4. Drain and dry the vine leaves. Wash the radicchio and break apart the leaves. Arrange radicchio and endive leaves on 4 small plates and place a vine leaf on top.

5. Place the cooked cheese on top of the vine leaf and spoon some of the oil mixture over each serving.

TIME: Preparation takes 20 minutes, cooking takes about 5 minutes.

BUYING GUIDE: Packaged vine leaves are now available in many supermarkets. If you cannot buy them there, try a health food shop or delicatessen.

STUFFED COURGETTES

In Greece, when stuffed vegetables are served with a sauce, it is usually a lemon-egg mixture. Try the sauce with peppers or vine leaves, too.

SERVES 4

4 medium-sized courgettes

Stuffing

1 small onion, finely chopped
30g/1oz butter or margarine
120g/4oz minced lamb or beef
1 tsp ground cumin
1 tsp chopped oregano
2 tsps chopped fresh parsley
2 tsps chopped fresh fennel fronds
60g/2oz cooked long-grain rice
2 tbsps grated cheese
Salt and pepper

Egg and Lemon Sauce

2 egg yolks
1 lemon
Salt and pepper

1. Wash the courgettes well and top and tail them. Using a swivel vegetable peeler, apple corer or a small baller, scoop the middle out of the courgettes, being careful not to damage the outer skins. Leave a thin margin of flesh on the inside for support. Alternatively, slice lengthwise and scoop out the middle.

2. Place the courgettes in boiling, salted water and parboil for about 2 minutes. Rinse immediately in cold water and leave to drain.

3. Prepare the stuffing by softening the onions in half of the butter until they are just transparent. Add the meat and cook until just beginning to brown. Chop up the reserved courgette flesh and add it to the meat. Mix with the remaining stuffing ingredients.

4. Mix the stuffing well and fill the hollow in each courgette using a teaspoon.

5. Melt the remaining butter in a large frying pan and, when foaming, place in the courgettes in a single layer. Add water to the pan to come halfway up the sides of the vegetables and cover the pan. Cook over gentle heat for about 20 minutes, basting the courgettes occasionally. Add more water during cooking as necessary.

6. When the courgettes are tender, remove them to a serving dish and keep them warm. Reserve about 60-90ml/4-6 tbsps of the liquid in the pan.

7. To prepare the sauce, beat the egg yolks and the lemon juice together until slightly thickened. Add some of the hot cooking liquid to the eggs and lemon juice and then return the mixture to a small saucepan. Cook over gentle heat, whisking constantly until slightly thickened. Strain over the courgettes before serving. Garnish with sprigs of fresh herbs if wished.

TIME: Preparation takes about 30 minutes, cooking takes about 20 minutes.

SERVING IDEAS: Stuffed vegetables may be served as a side dish or a starter. The courgettes may be served cold without the sauce.

WATCHPOINT: Do not allow the sauce to boil once the eggs have been added as it will curdle.

SPICED MEAT POTS

These delicious little meat pots make an excellent starter or light lunch.

SERVES 4

450g/1lb cooked beef, pork or veal, diced
570ml/1 pint beef stock
¼ tsp cinnamon
¼ tsp nutmeg
¼ tsp ginger
1½ tbsps thyme
1 tbsp Worcestershire sauce
Salt and pepper
Pinch of cayenne pepper
1 tbsp chopped parsley
2 hard-boiled eggs, chopped
450g/1lb unsalted butter
Small bay leaves

1. Simmer the meat in the stock until very soft. Mash with a fork and beat in the spices, thyme, Worcestershire sauce, salt, pepper and cayenne pepper.

2. Fold in the parsley and the hard-boiled eggs, being careful not to break up the eggs. Spoon the mixture into ramekins and chill.

3. Melt the butter, then turn up the heat until the butter boils, but does not brown. Watch it carefully. Remove from the heat and set aside until the butter fats sink to the bottom and the oil rises to the top. Slowly pour off the clearer oil, leaving the milky fat sediments behind.

4. Spoon a layer of clarified butter over the surface of the potted meats. Chill until set. Garnish with bay leaves, then add more butter to completely cover the meat. Chill until ready to serve.

TIME: Preparation takes about 1 hour, plus chilling time.

SERVING IDEAS: Serve with toast, or crusty bread and a salad.

COOK'S TIP: If the butter layer is unbroken, the potted meats will keep fresh for several days.

PÂTÉ AUX HERBES

A variety of herbs and spices accentuate the meat perfectly in this richly flavoured pâté.

SERVES 4

325g/11oz packet frozen spinach
450g/1lb pork, finely minced
1 onion, chopped
2 cloves garlic, crushed
2 tbsps finely chopped fresh basil
2 tbsps chopped parsley
Freshly grated nutmeg
½ tsp sage
Pinch cayenne pepper
140ml/¼ pint double cream
Salt and freshly ground pepper
225g/8oz leg or shoulder ham
225g/8oz rashers of streaky bacon, rind
    removed
1 egg, lightly beaten

1. Cook the spinach in boiling salted water for 5 minutes. Drain, and press between two plates to remove excess water. Chop finely and mix with the pork.

2. Combine the onion, garlic, herbs and spices, cayenne pepper, cream, and salt and pepper. Cut the ham into strips.

3. Line the bottom and sides of an ovenproof tureen with the rashes of streaky bacon.

4. Mix the pork and spinach into the cream mixture, add the egg and stir thoroughly. Press one-third of the mixture into the tureen. Add half the ham strips. Repeat until all ham and mixture is used up.

5. Cook in a preheated 180°C/350°F/Gas Mark 4 oven for 45 minutes, until set and cooked through. Remove from oven, cool, and serve sliced.

TIME: Preparation takes 20 minutes, cooking takes 1 hour.

SERVING IDEAS: Accompany with melba toast or crusty granary bread.

CHICKEN SATAY

This recipe makes a delicious starter or party dish.

MAKES 12-16 SKEWERS

1 x 1.6kg/3½lb chicken

Marinade

2 tbsps mild curry powder

2 cloves garlic, crushed

1½ tbsps sugar

2 tbsps oil

1 tbsp soy sauce

3 tbsps coconut milk (buy 1 large tin and
    use the rest for the sauce), warmed then
    cooled

1 tbsp lemon juice

Satay Sauce

8 dried red chillies or 2 tsps chilli powder

2 tbsps mild curry powder

3 tbsps oil (sunflower, corn or groundnut)

225g/8oz onions, finely chopped

2 cloves garlic, crushed

2 stalks fresh lemon grass or 1 tbsp lemon
    grass powder

340g/12oz salted roasted peanuts, finely
    chopped

140ml/¼ pint water

1 large tin coconut milk

2 tbsps peanut butter

2 tbsps dark soy sauce

60g/4 tbsps sugar

3 tbsps lemon juice

1. Skin and bone the chicken and cut into bite-sized pieces.

2. Mix the marinade ingredients together and pour over chicken pieces. Cover with foil or cling film and leave to marinate in the refrigerator for 3 hours.

3. Thread onto 12-16 bamboo skewers.

4. To prepare the sauce, deseed and soak dried chillies in hot water for 20 minutes, then finely chop. Mix curry powder, (and lemon grass powder and chilli powder, if used) into a thick paste with a little hot water.

5. Heat the oil in a saucepan, gently sauté the onion, garlic, chillies, and lemon grass until soft but not coloured. Add curry paste and continue cooking for another 2 minutes.

6. Add peanuts, water and remaining coconut milk, bring gently to the boil, add the remaining ingredients and return to the boil, stirring all the time. Simmer for about 5 minutes until the oil separates from the sauce, then remove from the heat.

7. Heat the grill to hot and quickly grill the chicken on the skewers, turning often, until golden.

8. Serve with the satay sauce and chunks of cucumber. Before eating, dip the skewers into the sauce.

TIME: Preparation takes about 40 minutes for the chicken plus 3 hours marinating. Sauce takes about 30 minutes to complete. Satays take about 10 minutes to cook.

HERBY GOAT CHEESE

Fresh goat's cheese is very popular in France, and is becoming more popular in other parts of the world. Its sometimes bland flavour is enlivened by the addition of herbs in this recipe.

SERVES 4

2 fresh goat cheeses
1 tbsp mixed fresh herbs, such as chives,
    parsley and chervil
1 tbsp finely chopped onion and shallot
10 capers
5 peppercorns
Salt and pepper
Few drops vinegar
Few drops lemon juice
½ tsp olive oil

1. Mix the cheeses with the chopped herbs, onion and shallot.

2. Mix in the capers, peppercorns and the salt and pepper.

3. Stir in the vinegar, lemon juice and olive oil. Stir well.

4. Place the cheese into 4 small ramekins, pushing it down well, and then set in the refrigerator for approximately 2 hours.

5. Turn out just before serving.

TIME: Preparation takes about 15 minutes plus 2 hours refrigeration.

SERVING IDEAS: Serve with a mixed salad tossed in vinaigrette sauce.

COOK'S TIP: Use only fresh goat cheese; avoid the dry variety which is often available, as it will crumble and will not mix well.

PASTA WITH FRESH BASIL SAUCE

The fresh basil sauce is made by pounding basil leaves with garlic, Parmesan and olive oil using a pestle and mortar.

SERVES 4

450g/1lb fresh pasta
20 fresh basil leaves
1 clove garlic
2 tbsps freshly grated Parmesan
60ml/2 fl oz olive oil
30g/1oz butter
Salt and pepper

1. Cook the pasta in salted, boiling water. Drain, rinse and then set aside to drain well.

2. Pound the basil leaves in a mortar and pestle, then add the garlic and pound until well mixed.

3. Add the Parmesan and continue to pound.

4. Transfer the mixture to a large bowl and whisk in the olive oil.

5. Add the butter to the pasta, place over a gentle heat and add the basil sauce. Stir well with a wooden spoon, and season with salt and pepper. Serve as soon as the pasta is heated through completely.

TIME: Preparation takes about 25 minutes and cooking takes approximately 8 minutes.

VARIATIONS: The sauce can be made in a food processor by adding all the ingredients together and processing until smooth. This reduces the preparation time to about 3 minutes.

SERVING IDEAS: Add pine nuts to the finished dish.

CHIVE CRÊPES WITH COTTAGE CHEESE AND 'CAVIAR'

These crêpes make a delicious lunch or supper dish. If wished, halve the quantities and serve as a starter.

MAKES 8-10 CRÊPES

120g/4oz plain flour
Salt
1 egg
1 tbsp oil, melted butter or margarine
280ml/½ pint milk
15g/4 tbsps snipped chives
Pinch cayenne pepper
Oil for frying

Filling
450g/1lb small curd cottage cheese
Salt and pepper
2 tbsps chopped parsley

Topping
60g/2oz melted butter
Red or black lump fish roe

1. Sift the flour with a pinch of salt into a deep bowl. Make a well in the centre of the flour and break an egg into the well. Add the oil and pour in half the milk.

2. Begin beating, gradually drawing in the flour from the sides slowly adding the remaining milk. Stir in the chives and cayenne pepper.

3. Allow the batter to stand for 30 minutes before using. Add more milk if the batter thickens too much on standing. It should be the consistency of whipping cream.

4. Brush a little oil on a small frying pan or crêpe pan and place the pan over high heat.

5. When hot, pour in a large tablespoonful of batter. Quickly tilt the pan to cover the bottom evenly with the batter.

6. Cook over a moderate heat until the edges are lightly browned. Lift with a palette knife and turn the crêpe over.

7. Cook the other side and stack the crêpes on a plate and keep covered while cooking the others. The batter makes about 8-10 crêpes.

8. Mix filling ingredients and spread on each crêpe. Roll up or fold in triangles and place in an oven-proof dish.

9. Drizzle over the melted butter, cover and heat through at 160°C/325°F/Gas Mark 3 for 15 minutes. Top with fish roe and serve.

TIME: Preparation takes 30 minutes and cooking takes about 30 minutes.

COOK'S TIP: If you have a food processor or blender, combine flour, salt, egg, oil and milk together and process until smooth to make the batter.

TO FREEZE: Crêpes freeze very well. Interleave them with greaseproof or silicone paper before freezing to stop them all sticking together.

SEVICHE

Do not be put off by the thought of eating raw fish, as the acid in the spicy marinade will 'cook' it. The result is delicious and well worth the wait.

SERVES 4

450g/1lb fresh cod fillets, skinned
Juice and grated rind of 2 limes
1 shallot, chopped
1 green chilli, seeded and finely chopped
1 tsp crushed coriander seeds
1 small green pepper
1 small red pepper
4 spring onions, chopped
2 tbsps olive oil
1 tbsp chopped parsley
1 tbsp chopped fresh coriander
Salt and pepper
1 small lettuce

1. Cut the cod fillets into very thin strips across the grain. Put into a bowl and pour over the lime juice and rind.

2. Add the shallot, chilli, crushed coriander seeds and cover the bowl. Leave in the refrigerator for 24 hours, stirring occasionally.

3. When ready to serve, thinly slice the peppers and spring onions.

4. Drain the fish and stir in the oil. Add the peppers, spring onions, herbs and salt and pepper and toss together. Shred the lettuce and arrange on serving plates. Top with seviche to serve.

TIME: Preparation takes about 20 minutes, plus 24 hours refrigeration.

VARIATIONS: Substitute monkfish, sea bass, haddock or salmon fillets for the cod.

SERVING IDEAS: Serve with crusty French bread or tortilla chips.

NOODLES IN CURRY SAUCE

This dish is certainly out-of-the-ordinary, but it tastes wonderful.

SERVES 4

450g/1lb thin egg noodles
30g/1oz butter or margarine
1 medium onion, finely chopped
1 clove garlic, crushed
2 tsps ground coriander
1 tsp ground fenugreek
1 tsp ground cumin
1 tsp ground turmeric
Pinch cayenne pepper
1-2 bananas peeled and sliced
Juice of ½ lime
280ml/½ pint stock
280ml/½ pint whole milk yogurt
2 tsps chopped mint
Salt and pepper

1. Cook the noodles in boiling, salted water until tender. Rinse under hot water and leave to drain.

2. Melt the butter or margarine in a large saucepan. Add the onion and cook to soften.

3. Add the garlic and spices and cook for 1 minute. Add the bananas and lime juice. Cook to soften the bananas slightly, mashing with a fork.

4. Pour on the stock, cover and cook for 20 minutes.

5. Blend the mixture in a food processor or liquidiser, until smooth. Return to the rinsed-out pan and bring back to the boil. Take off the heat and add the yogurt, mint, salt and pepper.

6. Pour the sauce over the noodles and toss before serving.

TIME: Preparation takes 15 minutes, cooking takes 20 minutes.

BUYING GUIDE: Plain whole milk yogurt is the natural thick-set type normally found in large pots for cooking.

LENTIL KEDGEREE

This delicious recipe combines spiced rice with lentils and onion to make a substantial vegetarian lunch or supper dish.

SERVES 4

225g/8oz basmati rice
225g/8oz red lentils
700ml/1¼ pints warm water
120g/4oz butter, or olive oil
1 medium onion, chopped
½ tsp crushed fresh root ginger
½ tsp crushed garlic
2.5cm/1-inch piece cinnamon stick
6 cloves
1 bay leaf
1 tsp ground coriander
¼ tsp ground turmeric
½ tsp freshly ground sea salt
2 green chillies, sliced in half lengthways

1. Wash the rice and the lentils thoroughly in cold water. Drain well.

2. Put the drained rice and lentils into a large bowl and cover with the warm water. Soak for 30 minutes, then drain very thoroughly, reserving the water.

3. Heat the butter or olive oil in a large saucepan. Stir in the onion and sauté gently for 2-3 minutes, stirring to prevent it burning.

4. Add the ginger, garlic, cinnamon stick, cloves and bay leaf to the onion and continue cooking for 1 minute.

5. Add the rice and lentils to the fried onion, along with the coriander, turmeric, salt and chillies. Stir over the heat for 2-3 minutes, until the rice and lentils are evenly coated with fat.

6. Pour the reserved water into the rice mixture and bring to the boil. Reduce the heat and cover the pan with a tight-fitting lid. Simmer for 12-15 minutes without stirring, or until the water has been completely absorbed.

7. Stir the rice and lentils together, remove and discard the chillies, and serve immediately.

TIME: Preparation takes 15 minutes, plus 30 minutes soaking time. Cooking takes approximately 20 minutes.

WATCHPOINT: Great care must be taken when using fresh chillies. If any of the juice gets into your mouth or eyes, rinse with lots of cold water.

VARIATIONS: Add smoked mackerel or canned tuna, for a non-vegetarian meal, and heat through.

COLD CHICKEN IN TARRAGON SAUCE

This recipe is ideal for a summer lunch or supper party as it can be prepared well in advance.

SERVES 6-8

1 × 1.5kg/3½lb chicken with giblets
Salt and pepper
Fresh tarragon

1 onion, quartered
1 carrot, quartered
1 stick celery, quartered
1 bay leaf

Sauce
60g/2oz butter
60g/2oz flour
Glass white wine or cider
1 tsp chopped tarragon
2 tsps chopped parsley
Juice of ½ lemon
3 heaped tbsps whipped cream
3 heaped tbsps mayonnaise

1. Generously sprinkle the inside of the chicken with salt, pepper and tarragon.

2. Place the onion, carrot and celery in a saucepan just large enough to hold the chicken snugly. Add giblets.

3. Place the chicken on top and pour over enough water just to cover. Cover the pan tightly and bring to the boil. Reduce heat and simmer for 1 hour.

4. Remove the pan from the heat and carefully turn the chicken breast-side down in the stock, taking care not to break the skin. Cover again and allow to cool.

5. Skin the chicken and remove all the flesh from the bones, slicing the meat from the legs into longish slivers and dividing the white parts up into similar-sized pieces.

6. Melt the butter in a heavy saucepan. Stir in the flour and cook for a minute or two. Add the white wine, then gradually stir in 280ml/½ pint of the chicken stock.

7. Add the chopped tarragon, parsley and lemon juice and bring the sauce to the boil. Cook for a further 2 minutes, stirring constantly.

8. Remove from the heat and allow to cool slightly before folding in the whipped cream and finally, the mayonnaise.

9. Toss the chicken pieces in about three quarters of the sauce and pile them into a large, shallow serving dish. Coat with the remainder of the sauce and garnish with tarragon sprigs and strips of lemon rind before serving.

TIME: Preparation takes 45 minutes and cooking takes about 1 hour 20 minutes.

COOK'S TIP: Poach the chicken the day before you need it, then refrigerate overnight.

FRESH PASTA WITH GARLIC AND PARSLEY

Cooked fresh pasta served in butter, olive oil, garlic and parsley sauce.

SERVES 4

450g/1lb fresh pasta
60g/2oz butter
2 cloves garlic, finely chopped
Few drops olive oil
2 tbsps parsley, finely chopped
Salt and pepper

1. Cook the pasta to your liking in salted, boiling water. Rinse in hot water and set aside to drain.

2. Melt the butter in a frying pan, stirring well mix in the garlic. Cook for a few minutes.

3. Add the drained pasta to the pan, add the garlic and fry for 1 minute.

4. Add a few drops of olive oil to the pan, remove from the heat and sprinkle over the parsley. Season with salt and pepper and serve.

TIME: Preparation takes about 5 minutes and cooking takes approximately 15 minutes.

COOK'S TIP: Mix together the butter, garlic and parsley. Keep in the refrigerator and use it for this dish when unexpected guests arrive.

VARIATIONS: If preferred, the butter may be substituted with olive oil.

STUFFED BREAST OF LAMB

Breast of lamb is an inexpensive cut, which makes a good meal when boned, rolled and stuffed.

SERVES 4

Half breast of lamb
1 medium onion
Salt and pepper
120g/4oz white breadcrumbs
60g/2oz chopped suet
½ tsp marjoram
½ tsp thyme
Grated rind of half a lemon
Salt and pepper
1 egg
1 tbsp flour

1. Bone the breast of lamb with a sharp knife and trim off excess fat. Place the bones in a saucepan with half the onion and some salt and pepper. Cover them with water, bring to the boil, skim, cover the pot and simmer for 30 minutes.

2. Mix the breadcrumbs, suet, herbs, lemon rind, a little salt and pepper and the remaining onion, finely chopped, and bind them with the egg. Add 2-3 tbsps of the bone stock and spread the stuffing on the breast of lamb.

3. Roll up, starting at the wide end. Tie up firmly with string and place in a greased roasting tin. Bake in the oven, 200°C/400°F/ Gas Mark 6, for about 1 hour or until tender.

4. Transfer the meat to a serving dish and keep hot while you make the gravy. Drain off any excess fat from the roasting tin, retaining about 2 tbsps. Stir in the flour and heat until the mixture browns.

5. Stir in about 280ml/½ pint of the stock. Bring to the boil, stirring constantly. Boil for a few minutes and then strain into a gravy boat and serve with the stuffed lamb.

TIME: Preparation takes 15 minutes and cooking takes about 1 hour 40 minutes.

COOK'S TIP: Roast the lamb for about 20-25 minutes per 450g/1lb (including stuffing).

SERVING IDEAS: Serve with new potatoes and courgettes.

SWORDFISH STEAKS WITH GREEN PEPPERCORNS AND GARLIC SAUCE

Swordfish steaks are delicious and are now easily available at most good fishmongers.

SERVES 4

2 tbsps fresh green peppercorns
90ml/6 tbsps lemon juice
60ml/4 tbsps olive oil
Freshly ground sea salt
4 swordfish steaks
1 egg
1 clove garlic, roughly chopped
140ml/¼ pint oil
2 tsps fresh oregano leaves, finely chopped
Salt and freshly ground black pepper

1. Crush the green peppercorns lightly using a pestle and mortar.

2. Mix the lemon juice, olive oil and salt into the lightly crushed green peppercorns.

3. Place the swordfish steaks in a shallow ovenproof dish and pour the lemon and oil mixture over each steak. Refrigerate overnight, turning occasionally until the fish becomes opaque.

4. Using a blender or food processor, mix together the egg and garlic.

5. With the machine still running, gradually pour the oil through the funnel in a thin steady stream into the egg and garlic mixture. Continue to blend until the sauce is thick.

6. Preheat the grill to hot and arrange the swordfish on the grill pan.

7. Sprinkle the chopped oregano over the swordfish steaks and season well. Cook for 15 minutes, turning them frequently and basting with the lemon and pepper marinade.

8. When the steaks are cooked, place onto a serving dish and spoon the garlic mayonnaise over to serve.

TIME: Preparation takes 25 minutes, plus overnight marinating. Cooking takes about 15 minutes.

VARIATIONS: Substitute 2 tbsps well rinsed canned green peppercorns in place of the fresh peppercorns if you cannot get these, and use tuna steaks instead of the swordfish if you prefer.

SERVING IDEAS: Serve with jacket potatoes and fresh salad.

47

RABBIT IN MUSTARD SAUCE

Fresh and frozen rabbit is now available in many supermarkets and makes an excellent change from chicken and beef.

SERVES 4

1 × 1.8kg/4lb rabbit, cleaned and cut into
   serving pieces
60ml/4 tbsps French mustard
30g/1oz butter
1 tbsp oil
1 medium onion, finely chopped
30g/1oz plain flour
1 scant tsp dried thyme
1 scant tsp rosemary
430ml/¾ pint dry cider
Salt and freshly ground black pepper

1. Smear the rabbit pieces with the mustard and set aside for a couple of hours to absorb the flavour.

2. Melt the butter and oil together in a large frying pan and when the foam subsides fry the rabbit pieces, a few at a time, until golden brown. Transfer them to a flameproof casserole.

3. Add the chopped onion to the frying pan, adding a little more oil if necessary. Fry until soft and then add the flour and herbs, stirring constantly.

4. Cook the onion and herbs for 1-2 minutes over gentle heat, then add the cider. Stir the sauce well and bring to the boil. Season to taste and pour the thickened sauce over the rabbit pieces.

5. Cover the casserole and simmer gently for 45 minutes-1 hour or until tender. Exact cooking time will depend on the age of the rabbit.

TIME: Preparation takes about 15 minutes plus a few hours marinating. Cooking takes 45 minutes-1 hour.

SERVING IDEAS: Serve with buttered noodles and a green salad or vegetable. French bread is also a handy accompaniment to mop up all the lovely juices.

VARIATION: Use 675-900g/1½-2lbs cubed rabbit meat, if joints are unavailable, and alter the cooking time accordingly.

Red Mullet with Herbs en Papillote

This impressive dish is perfect for entertaining.

SERVES 4

Oil

4 large red mullet, scaled, gutted and
    trimmed

60g/2oz butter

3 shallots, finely chopped

4 tbsps chopped herbs such as chervil,
    tarragon, marjoram, basil and parsley

60ml/4 tbsps dry white wine

Salt and pepper

Garnish

Lemon wedges or slices

1. Cut 4 circles of greaseproof paper large enough to enclose each fish. Brush with oil and place one fish on half of each piece of paper.

2. Melt the butter and cook the shallots to brown lightly. Allow to cool slightly and add the herbs, salt and pepper.

3. Pour 1 tbsp wine over each fish. Spoon the butter mixture on each fish and fold the other half of the paper or foil over the fish and seal the edges.

4. Place the parcels in a roasting tin or on a baking sheet with a lip around the edge in case the parcels leak. Cook in a preheated 180°C/350°F/Gas Mark 4 oven for about 20-25 minutes, depending upon the size of the fish.

5. Place the parcels on individual serving plates and allow each person to open their own just before ready to eat so that none of the flavour is lost. Serve with lemon wedges.

TIME: Preparation takes 20 minutes, cooking takes 20-25 minutes.

SERVING IDEAS: Serve with new potatoes and a green salad or mange tout and baby carrots.

ROAST PORK
IN WILD GAME STYLE

This recipe is Polish, where the love of game is part of the culinary history, so even meat from domestic animals is often given the same treatment.

SERVES 6-8

1 x 1.4kg/3lb boneless joint of pork
60g/4 tbsps lard or dripping
Paprika
1 tsp cornflour
175ml/6 fl oz sour cream or thick yogurt
1 tbsp chopped fresh dill

Marinade
1 carrot, finely chopped
2 celery sticks, finely chopped
1 bay leaf
5 black peppercorns
5 allspice berries
2 sprigs thyme
10 juniper berries, slightly crushed
2 onions, sliced
140ml/¼ pint dry white wine
Juice and grated rind of 1 lemon

Beetroot Accompaniment
60g/2oz butter or margarine
2 tbsps flour
1 onion, finely chopped
1 clove garlic, crushed
140ml/¼ pint chicken or vegetable stock
900g/2lbs cooked beetroot, peeled and
    grated or cut into small dice
White wine vinegar
Sugar, salt and pepper

1. First combine the marinade ingredients in a small saucepan and bring to the boil. Allow to cool. Place the pork in a casserole dish or bowl and pour over the marinade. Cover and refrigerate for two days, turning the meat frequently. Remove the meat from the marinade and wipe it dry with kitchen paper. Reserve the marinade.

2. Heat the lard or dripping in a roasting pan. Sprinkle the fat side of the pork with paprika, and brown the pork on all sides in the hot fat. Cook, uncovered, in a preheated 190°C/375°F/Gas Mark 5 oven for 2 hours and 15 minutes. Baste frequently with the pan juices. Pour marinade over after one hour's cooking.

3. Remove the pork from the pan and set aside. Skim any fat from the surface of the sauce and strain the vegetables and meat juices into a saucepan. Mix the cornflour, sour cream, and dill together and add to the pan. Bring just to the boil, turn down the heat and allow to simmer for 1-2 minutes.

4. To make the beetroot accompaniment, melt the butter in a heavy-based saucepan and add the flour and onion. Stir well and cook over moderate heat until light brown. Add the garlic and stir in the stock gradually.

5. Bring to the boil, add beetroot, sugar, salt and pepper and vinegar to taste and cook for 10 minutes over moderate heat. Stir occasionally to prevent it sticking.

6. To serve, slice the pork and pour over the sauce. Serve with the beetroot. Crackling can be removed and sliced separately to make carving easier.

SPICED SALMON STEAKS

A blend of spices and sugar makes this easy-to-prepare salmon dish very out of the ordinary.

SERVES 4

120g/4oz soft light brown sugar
1 tbsp ground allspice
1 tbsp mustard powder
1 tbsp grated fresh ginger
4 salmon steaks, 2.5cm/1-inch thick
1 cucumber
1 bunch spring onions
30g/1oz butter
1 tbsp lemon juice
2 tsps chopped fresh dill weed
1 tbsp chopped fresh parsley
Salt and pepper

1. Mix the sugar and spices together and rub the mixture into the surface of both sides of the salmon steaks. Allow the salmon steaks to stand for at least 1 hour in the refrigerator.

2. Meanwhile, prepare the vegetables. Peel the cucumber and cut into quarters lengthways. Remove the seeds and cut each quarter into 2.5cm/1-inch pieces.

3. Trim the roots from the spring onions and cut off some, but not all, of the green part, in one piece.

4. Put the cucumber and spring onions into a saucepan, along with the butter, lemon juice, dill, parsley and seasoning. Cook over a moderate heat for about 10 minutes, or until the cucumber is tender and turning translucent.

5. Put the salmon steaks under a preheated moderate grill and cook for about 5-6 minutes on each side.

6. Serve with the cucumber and spring onion accompaniment.

TIME: Preparation takes about 15 minutes, plus standing time of at least 1 hour, and cooking takes 12-15 minutes.

PREPARATION: The salmon steaks are ideal for cooking on an outdoor barbecue.

VARIATIONS: Substitute cod or haddock steaks for the salmon.

SAFFRON CHICKEN

The delicate colour and flavour of saffron enhances the taste of chicken and gives this dish a Mediterranean flavour.

SERVES 4

1 x 900g-1.4kg/2-3lb chicken
2 tbsps olive oil
Salt and freshly ground black pepper
1 small onion, finely chopped
1 clove garlic, crushed
2 tsps paprika pepper
8 tomatoes, skinned
300g/10oz long grain white rice
700ml/1¼ pints boiling water
Large pinch saffron strands or ¼ tsp ground
    saffron
175g/6oz frozen peas
2 tbsps chopped fresh parsley

1. Cut the chicken into 8 pieces using a sharp knife or cook's cleaver. Start by pulling the legs away from the body and cutting down in between the thigh joints and the body to sever them. Halve these portions by cutting through the joint holding the drumstick and thigh together.

2. Cut off the wings by cutting down through the breast towards the wing joints. Discard wing tips.

3. Cut the carcass horizontally in half by splitting along the natural break in the rib cage. Cut the breast portion in half lengthwise down the breast bone.

4. Remove the skin from the chicken joints by pulling and cutting with a sharp knife.

5. Heat the oil in a large casserole or frying pan, and fry the chicken, turning it frequently to brown evenly. Season with a little salt and pepper, then remove it from the pan and set aside.

6. Add the onion and garlic to the juices in the pan and cook slowly until softened but not coloured.

7. Add the paprika to the onion and fry quickly for about 30 seconds.

8. Cut the tomatoes into quarters and remove the cores and seeds. Chop the tomato flesh finely and add this to the casserole with the paprika and onions.

9. Cook for about 5-10 minutes to draw off the liquid from the tomatoes. The sauce mixture should be of a dropping consistency when this has been done.

10. Stir the rice, water and saffron into the tomato purée along with the browned chicken portions. Bring to the boil, reduce the heat to simmering, then cover the casserole tightly and cook for about 20 minutes.

11. Add the peas and the parsley to the casserole, stir well and continue cooking for a further 5-10 minutes, or until the rice is tender and all the liquid has been absorbed.

12. Serve very hot.

TIME: Preparation takes about 25 minutes, cooking takes 30-35 minutes.

WATCHPOINT: Stir the casserole frequently from step 11 to prevent the rice from sticking.

GRILLED PORK CHOPS WITH HERBS AND PINK PEPPERCORNS

This combination of herbs could also be used with lamb chops.

SERVES 4

4 pork loin chops, 2.5cm/1-inch thick
60g/2oz butter, softened
1 shallot, finely chopped
1 tbsp chopped parsley
1 tbsp chopped marjoram
1 tbsp chopped thyme
Leaves from 1 sprig rosemary
Squeeze lemon juice
1 tbsp pink peppercorns, drained if in brine

1. Trim some of the fat from the outside of the chops and snip the edges to prevent curling.

2. Combine all the remaining ingredients except the pink peppercorns. Spread ⅓ of the butter mixture over one side of the chops.

3. Grill slowly for 15-20 minutes on one side. Turn over and spread ⅓ of the butter on the other side. Grill again slowly for a further 15-20 minutes. Remove the chops and keep warm. Heat the remaining butter and add the pink peppercorns. Pour over the chops to serve.

TIME: Preparation takes 15 minutes and cooking takes 30-40 minutes.

COOK'S TIP: To check if the chops are cooked, make a small cut on the underside of one of the chops to check that they are not still pink. If not completely cooked, grill for another 5 minutes.

SERVING IDEAS: Serve with new potatoes and French beans.

BAKED STUFFED MACKEREL

Mackerel is a highly nutritious fish, with a rich meaty flesh. It is best grilled,
baked or fried, and served with a sharp sauce.

SERVES 4

60g/2oz butter or margarine
1 small onion, finely chopped
1 tbsp medium oatmeal
60g/2oz fresh wholemeal breadcrumbs
1½ tsps chopped fresh lemon thyme
1½ tsps chopped fresh parsley
Salt and black pepper
2-3 tbsps hot water, if required
4 mackerel, cleaned and washed
    thoroughly

1. In a large frying pan, melt the butter or margarine. Sauté the chopped onion until soft, but not coloured.

2. Add the oatmeal, breadcrumbs, herbs and seasoning to the onion, and mix well to form a firm stuffing, adding a little hot water to bind, if necessary.

3. Fill the cavities of the fish with the stuffing and wrap each one separately in well-greased aluminium foil.

4. Place each fish parcel in a roasting tin, or on a baking sheet, and cook in a preheated oven, 190°C/375°F/Gas Mark 5, for 30 minutes or until the fish is firm and flakes easily when tested with a knife.

TIME: Preparation takes about 15 minutes, and cooking takes
about 30 minutes.

VARIATIONS: The stuffing in this recipe is also delicious with
herrings or whiting.

SERVING IDEAS: Serve this dish garnished with fresh watercress
and new potatoes.

CHICKEN CACCIATORE

The use of herbs, wine and vinegar in this delicious Italian family meal gives a wonderful, hearty flavour. Serve with rice or pasta and a mixed salad.

SERVES 4-6

60ml/4 tbsps olive oil
1.4kg/3lbs chicken pieces
2 onions, sliced
3 cloves garlic, crushed
225g/8oz button mushrooms, quartered
140ml/¼ pint red wine
1 tbsp wine vinegar
1 tbsp fresh chopped parsley
2 tsps fresh chopped oregano
2 tsps fresh chopped basil
1 bay leaf
450g/1lb canned tomatoes
140ml/¼ pint chicken stock
Salt and freshly ground black pepper
Pinch of sugar

1. In a large frying pan heat the oil and add the chicken pieces, skin side down, in one layer.

2. Brown for 3-4 minutes, then turn each piece over. Continue turning the chicken portions until all surfaces are well browned.

3. Remove the chicken portions to a plate and keep warm.

4. Add the onions and garlic to the oil and chicken juices in the frying pan. Cook lightly for 2-3 minutes, or until they are just beginning to brown.

5. Add the mushrooms to the pan and cook for about 1 minute, stirring constantly.

6. Pour the wine and vinegar into the pan and boil rapidly to reduce to about half the original quantity.

7. Add the herbs, bay leaf and tomatoes, stirring well to break up the tomatoes.

8. Stir in the chicken stock and season with salt and pepper and sugar.

9. Return the chicken to the tomato sauce and cover with a tight-fitting lid. Simmer for about 1 hour, or until the chicken is tender.

TIME: Preparation takes about 30 minutes, cooking takes 1 hour.

VARIATIONS: Use the delicious sauce in this recipe with any other meat of your choice.

TO FREEZE: This dish freezes well for up to 3 months. Defrost thoroughly and reheat by bringing to the boil then simmering for at least 30 minutes before serving.

TARRAGON GRILLED RED MULLET

Red mullet is a very decorative little fish that is now readily available at fishmongers and supermarkets.

SERVES 4

4 large or 8 small red mullets, gutted, scaled, washed and dried
4 or 8 sprigs of fresh tarragon
60ml/4 tbsps vegetable oil
2 tbsps tarragon vinegar
Salt and freshly ground black pepper
1 egg
1 tsp Dijon mustard
120ml/4 fl oz sunflower oil
1 tbsp wine vinegar
1 tsp brandy
1 tbsp chopped fresh tarragon
1 tbsp chopped fresh parsley
1 tbsp double cream

1. Rub the inside of each mullet with a teaspoonful of salt, scrubbing hard to remove any discoloured membranes inside. Rinse thoroughly.

2. Place a sprig of fresh tarragon inside each fish.

3. Using a sharp knife cut 2 diagonal slits on the side of each fish.

4. Mix together the vegetable oil, tarragon vinegar and a little salt and pepper in a small bowl.

5. Arrange the fish in a shallow dish and pour over the tarragon vinegar marinade, brushing some of the mixture into the cuts on the side of the fish. Refrigerate for 30 minutes.

6. Put the egg into a blender or food processor along with the mustard and a little salt and pepper. Process for 2-3 seconds to mix.

7. With the machine running, add the oil through the funnel in a thin steady stream. Continue blending the dressing until it is thick and creamy.

8. Add the vinegar, brandy and herbs, and process for a further 30 seconds to mix well.

9. Lightly whip the cream with a small whisk until it thickens.

10. Fold the slightly thickened cream carefully into the oil and vinegar dressing. Pour into a serving dish and refrigerate until ready to use.

11. Arrange the fish on a grill pan and cook under a preheated hot grill for 5-8 minutes per side, depending on the size of the fish. Baste frequently with the marinade while cooking, then serve with a little of the sauce and some sprigs of fresh tarragon.

TIME: Preparation takes about 15 minutes plus 30 minutes marinating, cooking takes 10-16 minutes.

VARIATIONS: Use herrings or mackerel in place of the mullet.

LIVER WITH CORIANDER, LEMON AND PINE NUTS

Liver makes a very quick and nutritious meal. Serve this dish with creamed potatoes and a green vegetable.

SERVES 4

3 tbsps olive oil
450g/1lb calves or lambs liver, skinned, trimmed and cut into strips
1 large onion, thinly sliced
60g/2oz pine nuts
2 tsps ground coriander
2 tbsps lemon juice
Salt and pepper

Garnish
Fresh coriander leaves
Lemon slices

1. Heat the oil in a large frying pan. Add the liver and sauté quickly over high heat to seal. Remove the liver and keep it warm.

2. Add the onion and pine nuts and cook until golden.

3. Add the coriander and cook for 1-2 minutes over a low heat.

4. Return the liver to the pan and pour over the lemon juice. Season with salt and pepper and heat through for 1-2 minutes.

5. Serve garnished with fresh coriander and lemon slices.

TIME: Preparation takes 20 minutes and cooking takes 5-6 minutes.

COOK'S TIP: Do not overcook the liver else it will become tough.

VARIATIONS: Use ground cumin instead of ground coriander.

GRILLED SARDINES WITH LEMON AND OREGANO

Sardines taste wonderful in this simple recipe which uses lemon and oregano to bring out the full flavour of the fish.

SERVES 4-6

8-12 sprigs fresh oregano
8-12 fresh sardines, gutted, scaled, washed and dried
90ml/3 fl oz olive oil
Juice and rind of 2 lemons
Salt and pepper
1 tbsp dried oregano

1. Place one sprig of oregano inside each fish.

2. Mix oil, lemon juice and rind, salt and pepper together. Make two slits on each side of the fish and brush the fish with the lemon mixture.

3. Grill the fish over hot coals or under a grill for 3-4 minutes per side, basting frequently.

4. When the fish are nearly done, sprinkle the dried oregano on the coals. The smoke will give the fish extra flavour. If grilling in a conventional cooker, or if you prefer a stronger flavour, spinkle the oregano over the fish.

TIME: Preparation takes 15 minutes, cooking takes 6-8 minutes.

COOK'S TIP: When buying fish, ensure they have a bright eye and colour and are still firm.

MARINATED CHICKEN WITH WALNUT SAUCE

Offer your guests chicken in a walnut sauce, which tastes delicious and is very easy to make.

SERVES 4

2 × 900g/2lb chickens, cut in half

Marinade

140ml/¼ pint olive oil

Juice and grated rind of 2 lemons

1 tbsp chopped fresh oregano

Pinch ground cumin

1 tbsp chopped fresh parsley

2 tsps chopped fresh thyme

Salt and pepper

Pinch sugar

Walnut Sauce

2 cloves garlic, peeled and roughly chopped

4 slices bread, crusts removed, soaked in water for 10 minutes

2 tbsps white wine vinegar

60-70ml/4-5 tbsps olive oil

Salt and pepper

1-2 tbsps water (optional)

90g/3oz ground walnuts

1. Remove the backbones from the chickens with poultry shears. Bend the legs backwards to break the ball and socket joint. Cut away some of the ribcage with a sharp knife. Flatten the chickens slightly with a meat mallet or rolling pin.

2. Mix together the marinade ingredients in a large, shallow dish or a large plastic bag. Place in the chicken and turn to coat. If using a plastic bag, fasten securely and place in a dish to catch any drips. Refrigerate for at least 4 hours or overnight.

3. Place the chicken on a grill and cook under low heat for about 30 minutes, basting frequently. Raise the heat and cook for a further 10 minutes, skin side up, to brown nicely.

4. Meanwhile, place the garlic in a food processor and squeeze the bread to remove the water. Add the bread to the food processor along with the vinegar. With the machine running, pour the oil through the funnel in a thin, steady stream.

5. Add water if necessary to bring the sauce to coating consistency. Add salt and pepper and stir in the walnuts by hand. When the chicken is cooked, remove it to a serving dish and pour over any remaining marinade. Serve with the walnut sauce.

TIME: Preparation takes about 30 minutes plus at least 4 hours marinating time, cooking takes about 40 minutes.

COOK'S TIP: Add the oil to the vinegar very slowly.

SERVING IDEAS: Garnish with lemon wedges and sprigs of parsley or other fresh herbs, if wished. Serve with rice and a green or tomato salad.

LAMB KEBABS

Meat kebabs are a typical Greek dish and these have all the characteristic flavours – oregano, garlic, lemon and olive oil.

SERVES 4

675g/1½lbs lean lamb from the leg or neck fillet
Juice of 1 large lemon
90ml/6 tbsps olive oil
1 clove garlic, crushed
1 tbsp chopped fresh oregano
1 tbsp chopped fresh thyme
Salt and pepper
Fresh bay leaves
2 medium onions

1. Trim the meat of excess fat and cut it into 5cm/2-inch cubes. Mix together the remaining ingredients except the bay leaves and the onions. Pour the mixture into a shallow dish or into a large plastic bag.

2. Place the meat in the marinade and turn to coat completely. If using a bag, tie securely and place in a dish to catch any drips. Refrigerate, and leave to marinate for at least 4 hours, or overnight.

3. To assemble the kebabs, remove the meat from the marinade and thread onto skewers, alternating with the fresh bay leaves.

4. Slice the onions into rings and slip the rings over the meat on the skewers.

5. Place the kebabs on a grill pan and grill for about 3 minutes per side under a preheated grill. Baste the kebabs often. Alternatively, grill over hot coals. Pour over any remaining marinade to serve.

TIME: Preparation takes about 20 minutes plus at least 4 hours marinating time. Cooking takes about 3 minutes per side.

VARIATIONS: Rump or sirloin steak may be used in place of the lamb although the cooking time will have to be increased.

SERVING IDEAS: A Greek country salad and rice make good accompaniments. Kebabs may also be served with stuffed vegetables.

CHICKEN WITH 'BURNT' PEPPERS AND CORIANDER

'Burning' peppers is a technique for removing the skins which also imparts a delicious flavour to this favourite vegetable.

SERVES 4

2 red peppers, halved
1 green pepper, halved
60ml/4 tbsps vegetable oil, for brushing
1 tbsp olive oil
2 tsps paprika
¼ tsp ground cumin
Pinch cayenne pepper
2 cloves garlic, crushed
450g/1lb canned tomatoes, drained and
    chopped
3 tbsps fresh chopped coriander
3 tbsps fresh chopped parsley
Salt, for seasoning
4 large chicken breasts, boned
1 large onion, sliced
60g/2oz flaked almonds

1. Put the peppers, cut side down, on a flat surface and gently press them with the palm of your hand to flatten them out.

2. Brush the skin side with 2 tbsps of the vegetable oil and cook them under a hot grill until the skin chars and splits.

3. Wrap the peppers in a clean towel for 10 minutes to cool.

4. Unwrap the peppers and carefully peel off the charred skin. Chop the pepper flesh into thin strips.

5. Heat the olive oil in a frying pan and gently fry the paprika, cumin, cayenne pepper and garlic for 2 minutes, stirring to prevent the garlic from browning.

6. Stir in the tomatoes, coriander, parsley and season with a little salt. Simmer for 15-20 minutes, or until thick. Set aside.

7. Meanwhile, heat the remaining vegetable oil in a casserole and sauté the chicken breasts, turning them frequently until they are golden brown on both sides.

8. Remove the chicken and set aside. Gently fry the onions in the oil for about 5 minutes, or until softened but not overcooked.

9. Return the chicken to the casserole with the onions and pour on about 280ml/½ pint of water. Bring to the boil.

10. Cover the casserole and simmer for about 30 minutes, turning the chicken occasionally to prevent it from burning.

11. Remove the chicken from the casserole and boil the remaining liquid rapidly to reduce to about 90ml/3 fl oz of stock.

12. Add the peppers and the tomato sauce to the chicken stock and stir well.

13. Return the chicken to the casserole, cover and simmer very gently for another 30 minutes, or until the chicken is tender.

14. Arrange the chicken on a serving dish with a little of the sauce spooned over. Sprinkle with flaked almonds and serve any remaining sauce separately.

VEAL WITH SORREL AND CHEESE STUFFING

Fresh sorrel has a delightful flavour and is often found growing wild in the countryside or in old back gardens.

SERVES 6

---

1 x 900g/2lb rolled joint of veal
120g/4oz cream cheese with garlic and
　herbs
120g/4oz sorrel leaf, finely chopped
2 tsps fresh oregano or marjoram, chopped
60g/2oz finely chopped walnuts
Salt and freshly ground black pepper
60g/2oz plain flour
½ tsp paprika
1 egg, beaten
120g/4oz dried breadcrumbs
45g/1½oz unsalted butter, melted

---

1. Unroll the veal joint and trim off some of the fat from the outside, using a sharp knife.

2. Put the cheese, sorrel, oregano or marjoram, walnuts and salt and black pepper into a bowl. Mix together using a round bladed knife or your hands, until the ingredients are well bound together. Spread this filling over the inside of the veal.

3. Roll the veal joint up, swiss-roll fashion, and sew the ends together with a trussing needle and thick thread.

4. Dredge the veal roll with the flour and sprinkle with the paprika. Press this coating well onto the meat using your hands.

5. Brush the floured joint liberally with beaten egg and roll it into the dried breadcrumbs, pressing gently to make sure that all surfaces are thoroughly coated.

6. Place the coated veal on a baking sheet, brush with melted butter and roast in a preheated oven 160°C/325°F/Gas Mark 5, for 1-1½ hours, or until the meat is well cooked.

7. Allow to stand for 10 minutes before slicing and serving hot, or chill and serve cold.

TIME: Preparation takes 25 minutes, cooking takes 1-1½ hours.

VARIATION: Use a rolled joint of lamb instead of the veal.

SERVING IDEAS: Serve with salad or vegetables and a rich brown sauce.

POUSSINS WITH DEVILLED SAUCE

*Although this recipe takes quite a while to prepare, the end result is well worth it.
Serve with fresh cooked pasta and a large salad.*

SERVES 4

4 single (small) poussins
1 tsp each of paprika, mustard powder and
    ground ginger
½ tsp ground turmeric
¼ tsp ground allspice
60g/2oz butter
2 tbsps chilli sauce
1 tbsp plum chutney
1 tbsp brown sauce
1 tbsp Worcestershire sauce
1 tbsp soy sauce
Dash Tabasco sauce
3 tbsps chicken stock

1. Tie the legs of each poussin together and tuck the wing tips under the birds.

2. Put the paprika, mustard, ginger, turmeric and allspice, into a small bowl and mix together well.

3. Rub the spice mixture evenly on all sides of the four poussins, taking care to push some behind the wings and into the joints.

4. Refrigerate the poussins for at least 1 hour.

5. Arrange the poussins in a roasting pan. Melt the butter and brush it evenly over the birds. Roast in a preheated oven, 180°C/350°F/Gas Mark 4, for 20 minutes, brushing with the roasting juices during this time.

6. Put the chilli sauce, plum chutney, brown sauce, Worcestershire sauce, soy sauce and Tabasco and chicken stock into a small bowl and mix well.

7. Brush about half of this sauce over the poussins. Return to the oven and cook for a further 40 minutes.

8. Brush the poussins twice more with the remaining sauce mixture during this final cooking time so that the skins become brown and crisp.

TIME: Preparation takes about 15 minutes, plus 1 hour standing time.
Cooking takes 60-70 minutes, depending on the size of the poussins.

VARIATIONS: Use pigeons or grouse instead of the poussins in this recipe.

TO FREEZE: This dish freezes well for up to 3 months.

ROAST HERBED LEG OF LAMB

The next time you cook a leg of lamb for the Sunday roast, try this recipe for an interesting and delicious change.

SERVES 6

1 x 1.6kg/3½lb leg of lamb
2-3 cloves garlic
2 bay leaves
120g/4oz butter or margarine
225g/8oz wholemeal breadcrumbs
1 tsp chopped fresh thyme
1 tsp chopped fresh rosemary
1 tbsp chopped fresh parsley
Juice of 2 lemons
Salt and freshly ground black pepper

1. Prepare a sheet of foil large enough to wrap around the meat completely.

2. Peel and slice one or two of the garlic cloves. Make small cuts in the underside of the meat and insert the slices of garlic into this. Put the meat onto the foil with the bay leaves underneath.

3. In a small bowl, mix the butter thoroughly with the remaining ingredients. Spread this mixture over the upper surface of the meat, using a wet palette knife.

4. Loosely wrap the foil around the joint of meat, place in a roasting tin and roast in a preheated oven, 200°C/400°F/Gas Mark 6, for about 1½ hours.

5. Unwrap the foil and baste the joint with the melted fat that has collected in the base of the tin.

6. Continue roasting, uncovered, for a further 30 minutes, until the crust is brown and crisp.

TIME: Preparation takes about 15 minutes, and cooking takes about 25 minutes per 450g/1lb, plus 25 minutes extra. This may be reduced to 20 minutes per 450g/1lb, plus 20 minutes extra cooking, if you like slightly rarer meat.

COOK'S TIP: The breadcrumb mixture in this recipe is also delicious when used to coat a joint of gammon.

SERVING IDEAS: Serve with buttered new potatoes and seasonal vegetables.

POACHED SMOKED HADDOCK IN HERB SAUCE

This healthy dish makes an excellent mid-week meal served simply with boiled potatoes and a green vegetable.

SERVES 4

8 smoked haddock fillets of even size
Mixture of water and milk to cover the fish
Bouquet garni (1 bay leaf, 1 sprig thyme, 3
    parsley stalks)
6 black peppercorns

Sauce
45g/1½ oz butter or margarine
3 tbsps flour
280ml/½ pint milk
60ml/4 tbsps fresh mixed herbs, finely
    chopped
Salt and pepper
½ small bunch watercress leaves

1. Arrange the fish fillets skin side up in a large, shallow pan. Pour over enough water and milk mixed to cover the fish, and add the bouquet garni and peppercorns.

2. Cover the pan and bring the liquid almost to the boil. Leave the pan covered for 10-15 minutes to allow the fish to cook in the hot liquid. If the fillets are very thick it may be necessary to cook the fish a bit longer before leaving to stand.

3. Melt the butter for the sauce and, when foaming, stir in the flour. Cook to a very pale straw colour. Gradually pour on the milk, stirring continuously.

4. Remove the haddock to a serving dish and arrange skin side down on the plate.

5. Strain 280ml/½ pint of the fish cooking liquid and add to the sauce. Whisk the sauce well to blend thoroughly and add the herbs and the salt and pepper.

6. Stirring constantly, bring the sauce to the boil and allow to boil for about 2 minutes or until thickened. Combine with the watercress leaves in a food processor or blender and purée until the watercress leaves are finely chopped. If necessary, return to the pan to heat through.

7. Spoon some of the sauce over the haddock fillets and serve the rest separately.

TIME: Preparation takes 10 minutes, cooking takes 20 minutes.

VARIATIONS: Substitute your favourite white fish fillets if you don't like smoked fish.

BULGAR WHEAT SALAD

This is a Lebanese salad and it is very good for parties and picnics.

SERVES 6

225g/8oz bulgar or pourgouri (precooked, cracked wheat)
250ml/8 fl oz boiling water
8-10 spring onions, chopped
1 green pepper, chopped
120ml/8 tbsps chopped fresh parsley
2 tbsps chopped fresh mint leaves

Dressing

3 tbsps lemon juice
175ml/6 fl oz olive oil
1 tsp grated lemon rind
1 tsp ground mixed spice
½ tsp ground cumin
1 tsp salt
¼ tsp freshly ground black pepper

1 small iceberg lettuce, shredded
2 large firm tomatoes, cut into wedges
10-15 pitted black olives, halved
2-3 sprigs mint
1-2 sprigs fresh coriander

1. Place the bulgar into a bowl and add the boiling water. Cover and stand for 10-15 minutes.

2. Drain the bulgar by squeezing out the excess water.

3. Mix the spring onions, green pepper, parsley and mint with the bulgar.

4. Combine all the dressing ingredients in a screw top jar and shake well.

5. Pour the dressing over the bulgar mixture and mix lightly.

6. Line a platter with shredded lettuce. Place the prepared bulgar in the centre.

7. Garnish with the tomato, olives, mint and coriander leaves.

TIME: Preparation takes 1½-2 hours, including soaking time.

COOK'S TIP: Prepare the vegetables while the bulgar is soaking and use a food processor to chop the herbs.

HUNGARIAN SAUSAGE SALAD

This hearty salad is filling enough to be served as a main course.

SERVES 4-6

6 small potatoes

Dressing

140ml/¼ pint oil

3 tbsps wine vinegar

1 tsp Dijon mustard

1 tsp dill seeds, slightly crushed

1 tbsp chopped parsley

1 tsp chopped dill

Pinch hot paprika

Salt

450g/1lb sausage such as kielbasa, smoked
    pork sausage, knockwurst or bratwurst

1 large red onion, thinly sliced

2 green peppers, sliced

4 tomatoes, quartered

1. Scrub and peel the potatoes and cook in salted water in a covered saucepan for 20 minutes or until tender.

2. Mix all the dressing ingredients together in a medium-sized bowl.

3. Dice the potatoes while still warm and coat with the dressing. Leave the potatoes to cool in the dressing.

4. If using knockwurst boil for 5 minutes. Grill the bratwurst until evenly browned on all sides. Slice the sausage into 2.5cm/½-inch slices and combine with the onion, pepper and tomatoes.

5. Carefully combine the sausage mixture with the potatoes in the dressing, taking care not to over mix and break up the potatoes.

6. Pile into a large serving dish and allow to stand for 1 hour before serving.

TIME: Preparation takes 25 minutes, cooking takes 20-25 minutes. The salad tastes better if given 1 hour standing time, but this is optional.

VARIATION: If you prefer pepperoni, substitute it for the kielbasa.

CUCUMBER SALAD

This salad is Polish, and it is known by the name Mizeria – quite a gloomy word
for such a refreshing, delicious and versatile salad and side dish.

SERVES 6

1 large cucumber
140ml/¼ pint sour cream
2 tsps white wine vinegar
1 tsp sugar
1 tbsp chopped fresh dill
Salt and pepper

1. Wash the cucumber well. Trim off the thin ends of the cucumber.

2. Using a cannelle knife or the prongs of a fork, score the skin of the cucumber in long strips.

3. Cut the cucumber into thin slices and place in a colander. Sprinkle with salt and leave to drain for 30 minutes.

4. Rinse the cucumber well, to remove the salt, and pat dry.

5. Mix the remaining ingredients together in a large bowl and toss with the cucumber slices.

6. Arrange the cucumber in a serving dish and serve chilled.

TIME: Preparation takes about 30 minutes.

PREPARATION: Sprinkling cucumber lightly with salt and leaving it to stand will help draw out the moisture and keep the dressing from becoming watery. This also makes cucumbers easier to digest.

VARIATION: Other chopped herbs may be used instead of, or in addition to, the dill.

HERB RICE PILAFF

Fresh herbs are a must for this rice dish, but use whatever mixture suits your taste or complements the main course.

SERVES 6

2 tbsps oil
30g/1oz butter
175g/6oz uncooked long-grain rice
570ml/1 pint boiling water
Pinch salt and pepper
90g/3oz mixed chopped fresh herbs
 (parsley, thyme, marjoram, basil)
1 small bunch spring onions, finely
 chopped

1. Heat the oil in a large, heavy-based saucepan and add the butter. When foaming, add the rice and cook over moderate heat for about 2 minutes, stirring constantly.

2. When the rice begins to look opaque, add the water, salt and pepper and bring to the boil, stirring occasionally.

3. Cover the pan and reduce the heat. Simmer very gently, without stirring, for about 20 minutes or until all the liquid has been absorbed and the rice is tender.

4. Chop the herbs very finely and stir into the rice along with the chopped spring onions. Cover the pan and leave to stand for about 5 minutes before serving.

TIME: Preparation takes about 20 minutes and cooking takes about 20-25 minutes.

SERVING IDEAS: Serve as a side dish to any meat, poultry or game recipe.

COOK'S TIP: The rice must simmer very slowly if it is to absorb all the water without overcooking. Add extra water or pour some off as necessary during cooking, depending on how much liquid the rice has absorbed.

HERBED VEGETABLE STRIPS

Fresh vegetables and herbs make a delicious side dish to any meal.

SERVES 4

---

2 large courgettes, ends trimmed

2 medium carrots, peeled

1 large or 2 small leeks, trimmed, halved
    and well washed

120g/4oz walnuts

1 small onion, chopped

2 tbsps chopped parsley

2 tbsps fresh basil, torn

280-430ml/½-¾ pint olive oil

Salt and pepper

---

1. Cut the courgettes and carrots into long, thin slices with a mandolin, or by hand. A food processor will work but the slices will be short.

2. Cut the leeks into lengths the same size as the courgettes and carrots. Make sure the leeks are well rinsed in between all layers. Cut into long, thin strips.

3. Using a large, sharp knife, cut the courgette and carrot slices into long, thin strips about the thickness of two matchsticks. The julienne blade of a food processor will produce strips that are too fine to use.

4. Place the carrot strips in a pan of boiling salted water and cook for about 3-4 minutes or until tender crisp. Drain and rinse under cold water. Cook the courgette strips separately for about 2-3 minutes and add the leek strips during the last 1 minute of cooking. Drain and rinse the vegetables and leave with the carrots to drain dry.

5. Place the walnuts, onion, parsley and basil in the bowl of a food processor or in a blender and chop finely.

6. Reserve about 3 tbsps of the olive oil for later use. With the machine running, pour the remaining oil through the funnel in a thin, steady stream. Use enough oil to bring the mixture to the consistency of mayonnaise. Add seasoning to taste.

7. Place reserved oil in a large pan and, when hot, add the drained vegetables. Season and toss over moderate heat until heated through. Add the herb and walnut sauce and toss gently to coat the vegetables. Serve immediately.

TIME: Preparation takes about 30-40 minutes and cooking takes about 6-8 minutes.

SERVING IDEAS: Serve as a side dish with grilled meat, poultry or fish and prepare larger quantities for a vegetarian main course. Parmesan cheese may be sprinkled on top.

PREPARATION: The sauce can be prepared several days in advance and kept, covered, in the refrigerator. It can also be frozen for up to 6 months.

TOMATOES PROVENÇALE

Use fragrant herbs from the Provence region of France to complement sweet tomatoes, and no salt will be required to enhance their flavour.

SERVES 4

4 large ripe tomatoes
2 tbsps olive oil
1 clove garlic, crushed
2 × 1.25cm/½-inch-thick slices white bread,
   crusts removed
1 tbsp chopped parsley
2 tsps chopped thyme or marjoram
Freshly ground black pepper

1. Cut the tomatoes in half and carefully cut out the tomato pulp using a grapefruit knife.

2. Put the tomato pulp into a sieve and press out the juice using the back of a wooden spoon. Put the dry tomato pulp into a large bowl.

3. Mix the olive oil and garlic together. Brush both sides of the bread with this mixture and leave to stand for 10 minutes.

4. Using a sharp knife, chop the oiled bread and the herbs together until they are well mixed and fine textured. Stir this into the tomato pulp and add black pepper to taste.

5. Press the tomato filling into the tomato shells, piling it slightly above the cut edge.

6. Arrange the tomatoes on an ovenproof dish and grill under a low heat for 5 minutes.

7. Raise the temperature of the grill to high and brown the tomatoes on top for a few seconds. Serve at once.

TIME: Preparation takes 15-20 minutes. Cooking time takes 5 minutes.

COOK'S TIP: Prepare the tomatoes in advance and grill them just before serving.

SERVING IDEAS: Serve as an unusual side dish.

COURGETTE, PEPPER AND ONION KEBABS

These kebabs are perfect for barbecues and summer lunches.

SERVES 4

4-6 courgettes, ends trimmed
1 large onion
1 large green pepper
1 large red pepper
60ml/4 tbsps dry white wine
1 tsp thyme
2 tsps chopped parsley
1 tsp chopped chives
120g/4oz melted butter

1. Peel the courgettes with a swivel peeler for a striped effect. Parboil for 4 minutes. Refresh under cold water and cut into 5cm/2-inch pieces.

2. Quarter the onion and cut into large pieces, separating the layers. Cut the peppers in half and remove the core and seeds. Cut into pieces the same size as the onion and thread the vegetables onto skewers.

3. Melt the butter, add the wine and cook for 1 minute. Add the herbs, salt and pepper.

4. Brush the kebabs lightly with the butter mixture and grill 5-6 minutes per side. Check the kebabs continuously and brush frequently with the butter mixture.

5. When the courgettes are tender, remove to a serving dish and pour over the remaining butter.

TIME: Preparation takes 20 minutes, cooking takes about 10 minutes.
SERVING IDEAS: Serve with barbecued meats or fried or grilled chicken.

MANGE TOUT AND CAULIFLOWER WITH GINGER AND LEMON GRASS

Surprise and delight your family or guests with this exotic vegetable dish.

SERVES 4-6

1 head cauliflower, broken into very small florets
225g/8oz mange tout, ends trimmed
3 tbsps oil
2 tsps lemon juice
Pinch sugar
Salt and pepper
1 small piece ginger, finely chopped
1 piece lemon grass
1 tbsp chopped parsley

1. Cook the cauliflower in boiling, salted water for 1 minute.

2. Add the mange tout and cook a further minute. Drain and refresh under cold water. Leave to drain and dry.

3. Mix the oil, lemon juice, sugar and seasoning together and add the ginger.

4. Peel the outer layers from the lemon grass and use just the inner core. Slice thinly or chop finely. Mix with the dressing.

5. Add the parsley to the dressing and pour over the vegetables, tossing to coat well. Serve cold.

TIME: Preparation takes 20 minutes, cooking takes 2 minutes.

SERVING IDEAS: Serve with cold meats or quiches.

CUCUMBERS WITH DILL SAUCE

Pink, white and green makes a pretty combination in this vegetable side dish.

SERVES 4

1 large cucumber, peeled in strips to give a
     stripy effect
175ml/6 fl oz double cream
2 tsps dill seed
2 tsps chopped fresh dill
2 tsps pink peppercorns, drained if in brine
Salt

1. Cut the cucumber in quarters,
lengthwise. Remove the seeds and cut each
quarter into 5cm/2-inch pieces.

2. Cook in boiling, salted water for 2
minutes, drain and refresh under cold
water. Leave to drain completely.

3. When the cucumbers are dry, combine
the cream and dill seed in a small saucepan
and bring to the boil.

4. Allow to cook rapidly to thicken slightly.
Strain and stir in the chopped dill, pink
peppercorns and a pinch of salt. Combine
with the cucumbers. Serve immediately and
do not reheat.

TIME: Preparation takes 15 minutes and cooking takes 5 minutes.

COOK'S TIP: If pink peppercorns are unavailable, do not substitute with
black peppercorns. Use toasted pine nuts instead.

VARIATIONS: Try the sauce with other vegetables such as courgettes or
young broad beans.

CARAMEL CUSTARD WITH ORANGE AND CORIANDER

This is one of the best loved puddings in Spain. Fragrant coriander gives it new appeal and its flavour is marvellous with orange.

SERVES 8

175g/6oz sugar
90ml/6 tbsps water
3 small oranges
850ml/1½ pints milk
1 tbsp coriander seeds, crushed
6 eggs
2 egg yolks
175g/6oz sugar

1. To prepare the caramel, put the sugar and water in a heavy-based saucepan and bring to the boil over gentle heat to dissolve the sugar.

2. Once the sugar is dissolved, bring to the boil over high heat and cook to a golden brown, watching the colour carefully. Do not stir.

3. While the caramel is cooking, heat eight, lightly greased, ramekin dishes to warm them. When the caramel is brown, pour an equal amount into each dish and swirl the dish quickly to coat the base and sides with caramel. Leave the caramel to cool and harden in the dishes.

4. Grate the oranges and combine the rind, milk and crushed coriander seeds in a deep saucepan. Set the oranges aside for later use. Bring the milk almost to the boiling point and set it aside for the flavours to infuse.

5. Beat the eggs, yolks and sugar together until light and fluffy. Gradually strain on the milk, stirring well in between each addition. Gently pour the milk over the caramel in each dish.

6. Place the dishes in a bain-marie and place in a preheated 160°C/325°F/Gas Mark 3 oven for about 40 minutes, or until a knife inserted into the centre of the custards comes out clean. Lower the oven temperature slightly if the water begins to boil around the dishes.

7. When the custards are cooked, remove the dishes from the bain-marie and refrigerate for at least 3 hours or overnight until the custard is completely cold and set.

8. To serve, loosen the custards from the sides of the dish with a small knife and turn them out onto individual plates. Peel the white pith from around the oranges and segment them. Place some of the orange segments around the custards and serve immediately.

TIME: Preparation takes about 30-40 minutes, cooking time for the custards is about 40 minutes. The custards also need at least 3 hours refrigeration before serving.

CRANBERRY SNOW WITH MINT

This simple dessert, which is quick and easy to make, looks very effective when served.

SERVES 4

60g/2oz fresh or frozen cranberries
90g/6 tbsps granulated sugar
2 egg whites
140ml/¼ pint whipping cream
140ml/¼ pint natural yogurt
2 tbsps chopped fresh mint

Garnish
Whole sprigs fresh mint

1. Combine the cranberries and 2 tbsps of the sugar in a small, heavy-based pan. Cook slowly until juice forms and the cranberries soften. Set aside to cool completely.

2. When the cranberries are cool, whisk the egg whites until stiff but not dry.

3. Gradually whisk in the remaining sugar. Whisk well in between each addition of sugar until stiff peaks form and the egg whites are smooth and glossy.

4. Whip the cream until thick, and combine with the yogurt.

5. Fold the egg whites into the cream and yogurt mixture along with the cooled cranberries and the chopped mint. Do not over-fold, the mixture should look marbled.

6. Spoon into individual serving dishes and garnish with the whole sprigs of mint. Make and eat the same day.

TIME: Preparation takes 15 minutes.

VARIATIONS: Use blackcurrants instead of cranberries. Check sweetness of dish during preparation.

SERVING IDEAS: Serve in tall glasses with langues de chat biscuits.

SPICED CREAM CAKE

The perfect tea-time treat!

MAKES 1 CAKE

225g/8oz butter or margarine
340g/12oz light brown sugar
4 eggs
340g/12oz plain flour, sifted
1½ tbsps baking powder
1½ tsps ground cinnamon
½ tsp ground nutmeg
½ tsp ground allspice
¼ tsp ground cloves
Salt
220ml/8 fl oz milk

Filling

Grated zest of orange
280ml/½ pint cream, whipped with 1 tbsp
    sugar
60ml/4 tbsps thick sour cream or natural
    yogurt

1. Grease 3 x 20cm/8-inch round cake tins and line the bases with circles of greaseproof or waxed paper.

2. Cream the butter and sugar together until light and fluffy. Beat in the eggs one at a time, beating well in-between each addition.

3. Sift the flour with the baking powder, spices and salt.

4. Gradually add the flour mixture to the butter, sugar and eggs and beat just until smooth. Stir in the milk by hand.

5. Divide among the three prepared cake tins and bake in an oven preheated to 180°C/350°F/Gas Mark 4, for about 25 minutes.

6. Cool the cake in the tins on a rack for a few minutes and then loosen the cake from the sides of the pan and turn out onto the rack to cool. Fold all the filling ingredients together, and spread the bottom layer with half of the cream mixture. Repeat with the second layer and top with third layer. Dust the top with icing sugar.

TIME: Preparation takes 15 minutes and cooking takes 25 minutes.

COOK'S TIP: The cake is cooked when it springs back when touched lightly with a finger tip.

WATCHPOINT: If the cake mixture starts to curdle when beating in the eggs, add a tablespoon of the flour and beat well.

LEMON AND GINGER CHEESECAKE

This fresh, creamy-tasting cheesecake is full of wholesome ingredients.

SERVES 6-8

45g/1½oz butter or margarine, melted
30g/1oz soft brown sugar
90g/3oz wholemeal biscuits, crushed
175g/6oz low fat soft cheese
2 eggs, separated
Finely grated rind 1 lemon
30g/1oz soft brown sugar
140ml/¼ pint natural yogurt, or fromage frais
15g/½oz powdered gelatine
3 tbsps hot water
Juice ½ lemon
3 pieces preserved stem ginger, rinsed in warm water and chopped
60ml/4 tbsps thick natural yogurt, or fromage frais
Fine matchstick strips lemon peel, or twists of lemon, to decorate

1. Lightly grease an 18cm/7-inch flan dish.

2. Mix the melted butter with the soft brown sugar and the crushed biscuits. Press the biscuit crumb mixture evenly over the base of the dish.

3. Chill the biscuit base, for at least 1 hour, in the refrigerator.

4. Beat the soft cheese with the egg yolks, lemon rind and sugar. Stir in the yogurt.

5. Dissolve the gelatine in the water, and add this in a thin stream to the cheese mixture, stirring thoroughly, to incorporate evenly.

6. Stir in the lemon juice and put the cheese mixture to one side until it is on the point of setting.

7. Whisk the egg whites until they are stiff but not dry and fold these lightly, but thoroughly, into the cheese mixture together with the chopped stem ginger.

8. Spoon this mixture into the prepared flan dish, smoothing the surface level.

9. Chill the cheesecake for 3-4 hours until the filling has set completely. Swirl the natural yogurt over the top of the cheesecake and decorate with the strips of lemon peel, or lemon twists.

TIME: Preparation takes about 30 minutes, plus 1 hour chilling time. The finished dish requires 3-4 hours refrigeration before serving.

COOK'S TIP: The gelatine will dissolve more quickly if you sprinkle it onto the hot water in a small bowl, and stand this bowl in a larger bowl of hot water. Stir the gelatine to ensure that no grainy bits remain.

Thyme Sorbet

Fresh thyme which is still in flower is used to give a very delicate flavour to this sorbet.

SERVES 4

500ml/18 fl oz water
150g/5oz sugar
4 small sprigs fresh thyme in flower

1. Boil the water and sugar together until a reasonably thick syrup is reached – this will take about 15 minutes.

2. Remove from the heat and add the sprigs of thyme. Remove the thyme from the syrup after 2 minutes and drain the syrup through a very fine sieve.

3. Pour the syrup into an ice cream maker and set in motion.*

4. When the sorbet has crystallized spoon into a container and keep in the freezer until needed.

* If an ice cream maker is not available, pour the strained syrup into a shallow container and place in the freezer until partly frozen. Remove from freezer, and beat quickly but thoroughly, then return to the freezer until needed. Beat again for a smoother textured sorbet with smaller ice-crystals.

TIME: Preparation time is approximately 30 minutes and crystallizing the sorbet takes about 30 minutes to 1 hour in an ice cream maker – longer if using the freezer method.

VARIATIONS: Use different herbs to flavour the this type of sorbet.

WATCHPOINT: Do not allow the thyme to remain in the syrup for longer than 2 minutes; the flavour is transferred very quickly.

Index